Written by Linda Stallone
Illustrated by Joan Schooley

The Flood that Came to Grandma's House

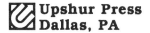
Upshur Press
Dallas, PA

Dedicated
to
Sally and Tony Stallone,
the real Grandma and Grandpa of the story,
and to their grandchildren,
Anthony and Maria, who inspired the book.

Library of Congress Cataloging-in-Publication Data

Stallone, Linda, 1947-
    The flood that came to grandma's house / written by Linda Stallone ;
illustrated by Joan Schooley.
        p. cm.
    Summary : When heavy rainfall causes the river to flood, Grandma
and Grandpa abandon their home and flee to higher ground.
    ISBN 0-912975-01-6 : $7.95
    [1. Floods--Fiction. 2. Grandparents--Fiction.] I. Schooley, Joan, ill.
II. Title
PZ7.S7836F1 1992
[E]--dc20   91-33955
                                                                CIP
                                                                AC

Printed in the United States.
Tallman Printing Co.
Forty Fort, Pennsylvania
Typesetting - Ola Mae Schoonover
Design Assistance - Annie Bohlin

This is Grandma and Grandpa's house.

They are sitting on their front porch watching the rain come down.

The rain came one day...

then two...

three days...

then four.

It rained longer and harder than it ever did before.

The puddles got bi**gger**.

The streams *ran faster.*

And the river rose... higher and higher.

Grandpa walked down to the river bank to see how high the water was rising.

He saw the water coming up the bank and said, "If it doesn't stop raining, the water will fill the river up so much that it will spill all over the ground and FLOOD the land on both sides of the river."

Grandpa helped lots of people fill bags up with sand.

They stacked the sand bags on top of each other all along the river bank.

They hoped the sand-bag wall would hold the river back where it was supposed to flow.

But the rain kept coming and the river kept rising higher.

The river got so strong and full of water that it was going to push through the sand-bag wall.

Everyone left the river bank to find safe places far, far from the water.

Since Grandma and Grandpa live close to the river, they jumped into their car to drive far, far away.

But Grandma said, "Stop! Stop! I forgot something."

What do you think was so important?

Grandma's clothes? her jewelry? her photo album?

NOPE.

Grandma ran back for Vanilla,

the biggest, furriest, whitest

cat in the whole wide world.

So off they drove to a friend's house—too far away for the river to reach them.

Meanwhile...

the river broke through the sand-bag wall.
Water flooded the streets.
Water started filling up the houses.

First the water filled Grandma's basement. Then the water went up the basement steps and filled the kitchen and the living room, getting higher and higher, going up the stairs to the bedrooms.

Before long the water went so high, all you could see was the roof of Grandma's house.

But everyone was safe, far from their houses,
far from the flood, too far to get hurt by the water.

Soon the rain stopped,
and the river water went
                          down
                                    down
                                              down
until water no longer spilled all over the ground.

The water was back in the river where it belonged.

Grandma and Grandpa went back to see their house.

What a yukky, muddy mess.

As the water went up

and then the water went down,

everything in the house floated around.

Everything got all mixed up and broken.

The dirty river water left a thick

layer of mud all over everything

the water touched—

And the water touched everything in the house!

Grandma and Grandpa sure had lots of work to clean up the mess. But many people came to help.

First, they threw everything that was in the house out onto the street.

Bulldozers
went up and
down the
streets,

pushed all
the piles of
muck

onto a
great
big
truck

and
took it
all away.

Grandma's house was empty. It took a long, long time to dry out.
It took a long, long, longer time to make it nice and clean again.
But everybody worked very hard.

The day finally came when Grandma and Grandpa
could live in their house again.

There they are now, sitting on their porch.
The house is clean and they are glad to be back.
This time I'll bet you can guess what they are talking about…   RIGHT!

The FLOOD that came to Grandma's house.
And they sure hope another flood never, never comes again.   AMEN